None of Us in White

Eve Alexandra

Winner of the Wilder Series Poetry Book Prize

Two Sylvias Press

Two Sylvias Press
PO Box 1524
Kingston, WA 98346
twosylviaspress@gmail.com

Cover Art: Neville Caulfield
Cover Design: Neville Caulfield and Kelli Russell Agodon
Book Design: Annette Spaulding-Convy
Author Photo: Greta Alexandra-Parker

Created with the belief that *great writing is good for the world*, Two Sylvias Press mixes modern technology, classic style, and literary intellect with an eco-friendly heart. We draw our inspiration from the poetic literary talent of Sylvia Plath and the editorial business sense of Sylvia Beach. We are an independent press dedicated to publishing the exceptional voices of writers.

For more information about Two Sylvias Press please visit:
www.twosylviaspress.com

First Edition. Created in the United States of America.

ISBN: **978-1-948767-24-8**

Praise for *None of Us in White*

Eve Alexandra's *None of Us in White* brilliantly mines the lover's condition, complicating its usual manifestations, romantic, filial, this work gathers through the human body itself. Alexandra's stunning collection offers a measured recklessness, guiding through immediate necessity: "What if we unlocked all the doors? What if we took the doors off the hinges?" Opening through this work, piercing between sense and atmosphere, human and animal, is an embodied current: "electric with desire, fireflies with luminous bellies." Alexandra's poetry pulses, a gorgeous voice, resounding between the collective and singular, where supposition bleeds into query, "Does the mouth make a sound for gun, arrow, berry, or flee?" Rooted and inspiring, *None of Us in White* illuminates, a queer erotics of a strongly lived and living feminist desire: "the slit of your sex, the coal of hooves, so close, for a second, as if you were nursing at my breast. Then you were off, leaping defiantly…," and so might we, through Alexandra's poetry of deep intimacy and wide scope, of careful reckoning into powerful wonder.

—**Ronaldo Wilson**, author of *Virgil Kills: Stories* and *Carmelina: Figures*

༚

Eve Alexandra's powerful new collection unlocks a sensual world that is acutely aware of its own potential for violence, pain, and heartbreak. Poem after poem is moving and unsettling. In the manner of Brigit Pegeen Kelly, here is a poet who can transport her readers into a world of charms, a place deer operate as sisters to the speaker, a realm that lists questions like transubstantiated miracles. The lushness of Alexandra's language is evident in landscapes filled with purple vetch, sumac, black-eyed Susans, bleeding hearts, and Queen Anne's lace. The intensity of emotion never lets up, and I was compelled to read and read and read. Always hoping for some relief for the speaker, for her to finally find peace and solid ground. When she says "I want to eat the whole wrecked world" I come to understand why. This collection touches a deep emotional truth and brims with significant interrogations and insight.

—**Didi Jackson**, author of *Moon Jar* and *My Infinity*

ॐ

Eve Alexandra's *None of Us in White* is an unflinching book of poems—a liturgy of love, wreckage, grief, and arrival that is as visceral as it is transcendent. Rooted in intimacy, in thrall with the natural world, and run through with a sequence of charms that offer as much warning as antidote, the range in these poems is stunning—in form and subject. Alexandra's materials—childhood, a father's presence and loss, bodily hunger—are made new in her hands. These poems are inventive and incantatory, their language precise and alive: "My hand runs the length of the field, and the field is your torso, odd rib that caught my heart like a lacy hem." Nature is mirror and medium, and love, a rebellion—"I am remembering how to make love. In protest." Lyrically beautiful, but also frank, surprising, and deeply moving, this is an extraordinary collection.

—**Kerrin McCadden**, author of *Landscape with Plywood Silhouettes* and *American Wake*

Acknowledgments

Grateful acknowledgment to the journals in which these poems first appeared:

"Derelict," *Barrow Street*
"Birthday Altar at Forty-Nine," "Loveland," and "Transubstantiation,"
   Cape Cod Review
"Crewel," "Velocity," and "Whitetail," *Green Mountains Review*
"Deer Tongue," "Mercy," and "Pastoral," *Hog River Press*
"Collision," *Hunger Mountain*
"Fish hook," *Narrative.*

Thank you to Kelli Russell Agodon and Annette Spaulding-Convy at Two Sylvias Press for this honor, for your careful attention, and giving my book a home.

Some poems come quick; others take years to write. I'm indebted to my family in both Vermont and Maine for all their love and support. I will be forever grateful to Julian Aiken, Kathryn James, Rachel DeWees, Mary Williams Engisch, and Kathleen Veslany for steadfast friendship that saved my life. I'm also grateful for the loyalty, grit, and humor of my sister-in-law Lora Wilson, and I miss her.

I want to thank my friends, colleagues, and students in the English Department and Gender, Sexuality, and Women's Studies Program at the University of Vermont. The Vermont School of Poets helped these poems along their way: Ben Aleshire, Jari Chevalier, Penelope Cray, Kristin Fogdall, Maria Hummel, Didi Jackson, Major Jackson, Kerrin McCadden, Holly Painter (for the title!), Alison Prine, Meg Reynolds, and Bill Stratton. Thank you in particular to Maria and Kerrin for their good counsel in all things poetry. I'm indebted to my friend Bill McDowell for the story in "Nest." Such a gift to have met you my poetry ally, John Bonnani. I want to thank Cole Barry for reading this manuscript so carefully, for your astonishing poems. Neville Caulfield, I adore your spirit, your dazzling eye. My teachers Mark Doty and Lynn Emanuel are always with me. And my deepest gratitude to the generous and brilliant Ronaldo Wilson, thank you for reminding me.

My father T. Michael Armstrong passed away in 2019. He was my constant, and this book and so many poems are in memory of him. Thank you to my stepmother Ellen Hagman who has been my good friend through so much change. To Mary Desranleau for Ptown. My dogs Romeo, Bodhi, and Arden, my daily heart. And thank you to Bill Kirchner who years ago issued the original deer tongue challenge when I had forgotten how to write a poem, for poetry club, and all that goes with it.

And most of all to my daughter, Greta Isabel Alexandra-Parker. Thank you. It is a gift to see you move through this world. You shine bright, you light my way.

In memory of my father T. Michael Armstrong

and

for Greta, my reason

Table of Contents

Brokenness, you do surprise me—

Carl Phillips

I.

Pastoral

My curls are weeping. *Oh little torso.* And sweat made by sleep.

                  Sting of nipple and braille of teeth. We are knee-deep

in the river. The cows need crossing. They muddy the water. They shit

  and they bite.

                    Waist deep in the purple vetch, there are honeybees

electric with desire, fireflies with luminous bellies.

                  Your tongue alive in my mouth. Our stars burn,

                      but never out.

In the north orchard, a tree wild with plums, sweet as the fruit

            between my legs. Your lips slick

                          with the taste.

I have been thinking about what it means to *have mercy.*

           How you have hurt me, but I am stitched to your ribs

                with butcher's string.

Call me *pretty*

same as that shepherd on a rope.

Sometimes I pass the time by pretending

I am your wife. I look out the car window and see a house. A door open.

A clothesline. Sheets for all the neighbors to see

like tiny acres of grief.

Moon Charm

Muzzle,
lilac, starling,
milk.

Derelict

Some nights after the dog has been walked
and the child is asleep, she takes off her clothes
and sits on the edge of the bed.

She sits still, wanting to feel
the way the body contains her, the slope
of her breasts, her shoulders,
neck like the bow of a ship,
hull of her ribs, folded sex,
a wilderness where she herself
has been lost, starved.

Each breath is a bird
burst from the rafters.
Who needs the jeweled glass,
the cross, the tiny shards
of a martyr's bone?

She puts her hand to her breast,
pinches a nipple. How it becomes flushed
and rosy between thumb and forefinger—perhaps
it is also thinking of the lost lover,
perhaps it waits for her tongue to return,
to be sucked on like a wild berry
or rock candy.

Is this prayer? Her breath,
each beat of her heart
like the swing of an axe.
When did love become violence?
When did she become a ghostly vessel?
In the poems she wrote as a girl, she was the siren,
titian hair cast like a net, song a bolt of silk.

She never imagined
she would be the wreck itself.
Hip like the hull of a ship, still as she can sit.
She caresses her belly,
remembers hiding the softness,
the awful roll of skin,
how her lover wanted to touch it,
so she relented,

offering both the best and least loved
parts of herself. These were things surrendered:
pride, shame.

When she walks in a room
she knows the men will look. They will not imagine
that a woman has done this to her.

Fish hook

The world is full of what I've lost.

September enters the Ausable,
the belly of the brook trout bright
as the wing of the monarch.

I consider telling you about these two fish
or the whole river of them. How they scissor
each other, how they flick and shimmer.

The first fishing line was made with spun silk.
The first lure of bronze or bone.
Daisy chain, spinner, decoy,
spoon.

Lure, yes, you would know
how to catch and clean such a thing,
separate the rainbow scales from the flesh.

Maybe you give this one back, catch
and release into the water.

Give it back like you did my body.

I'm trying to touch my lips,
but I can only come thinking of you.

Skin waxed the way you like it,
water everywhere, my nipples barbed,
your thumb rough

in my mouth.

Love Charm

I will make a wound
like a bed to sleep in.

Oology

When my daughter was young, I would scavenge for wild birds' eggs,
still with a bit of golden membrane, a tinge of blood,
robin's blue beyond the blue of a favorite ribbon tied in her braid.
There were speckled cardinal and mockingbird eggs.
I plucked quills from the carcass of a porcupine,
and discovered the jaw of a cow
walking the dog in a field of black-eyed Susans.

We kept our collection in an old bureau on the screened-in porch.
The bear tooth, and the miles of snakeskin my mother sent
in a shoe box from Florida. Nests too,
some tiny as saucers and the skeleton of a field mouse,
dainty as lace on the dress of a doll.
Rows of shells—great whelks and quahogs, oysters
from Long Island Sound unfit for pearls or mouths.
Our prize was the shell of a horseshoe crab
left behind one spring after breeding. Imagine
what it felt like to slip out of that armor, naked at last,
naked and dying.

I am no ornithologist, no biologist.
Why so obsessed with these little deaths?
When we were abandoned, my father and brother
drove down with a truck. I packed up
my girl and the dog. I wept for the dozens
of eggshells and the snakeskin we would not be taking.
I don't know if my daughter remembers—
she was seven. I had been a girl

                            of ether and air.

I wanted to tie us both to this earth.
I want to say it had something to do with promise
or permanence—

wherever you go darling, there will be a record.
There will be someone watching, cataloguing.
We can't help it.
We can't help but leave
sweet evidence.

The Bearded Iris

I. Rhizome

I had a dream of two girls in twin beds. We were sleeping. Tethered by the long gowns that tangled us. The water seeping in. Bucket. Dragline. The half knot has come undone.

One month after her death, purple irises bloomed. Then like a protest, two peach blossoms appeared. As if a twelve-year old girl had wept in bed and each petal a tear. This is how one goes to bed at twelve. Weeping. Petaled. Kneading linen.

You could see the sun set behind those petals, reverent and pale. Thin as the skin of a girl's satin slip, translucent as a newborn's skull. The plush fontanelle. Vernix. Lanugo. The language of new. The baby's head passes through the canal. We open like so many mouths. She sparkles. She crowns.

My sister curled into herself like an infant. Poison thinning her hair into bits of fluff. The shock of her skull lit up the room like a halo. I kissed her forehead. Twice. She said, *That's better.* She was moving away from us. Into the canal. Irises wild at the mouth of the river.

II. Barocco

I am remembering how to make love. In protest.

A lip is a blade. Stigmatic. Spathe. Anthers manufacturing pollen like a disco fairy drug. Her sex like the skin of a plum. She baked a black cherry pie. Pitted the small bodies with her thumb. I want to say sublime, but it was burlesque, all bump and grind, sweet and dirty on my tongue.

When I'm with you, she said, *I move into my male body.* All my lovers have fallen in between. Oh let's not dredge the rivers tonight. I'm wet. My cock is hard. This is happening. Simultaneously. I tried to explain to my sister why. My lover must wear a suit to the wedding. I have always wanted to be unveiled.

III. Transcendence

There are bones we have not fused. When I'm with you I move.

Virgin Charm
Birch bark,
rosary, lapis,
flame.

Junction

My city girl, she is new to the quiet. Slim stick
at seven, she is all blonde and honey,
smelling sweet and dirty like late summer berries,
ready to open. I am between
the wall and her body, back in my father's house
we lie in the narrow bed. I was a girl
raised in this village crisscrossed by trains.
I was just a girl when I fell in love with you.
Here the crickets sing like a chorus of persistent children
and the night is pierced by the bay of a mechanical hound.
The body we made between us is still breathing.
Empty bench, lonely platform, the revenant wail
lost in the sounds of coming and going. Once upon a time
we were beauty. Now
we're just the ones waving,
faded dresses, small and too familiar,
the smudge in your distance,
the echo to the whistle,
the soot and the pebbles,
the miles of track you ran over
and over again.

Mercy

I was done with voluptuous in more than one way. That winter odd cuts of meat were popping up on menus all over. Deer tongue, pork heart, and quail egg—ok not exactly flesh but somewhere within the yolk shining on Kate's polenta was the promise of someone—some cellular configuration of wing, of claw, breast and beak. For twenty years my mouth filled with food, my body with your tongue and hands, twins in utero sharing an impossible heart and one live beautiful girl. She was only seven and sleeping when you walked out the door. I was vomiting into the bathtub. Months later people we knew would stop me on the street and say, *You're melting*. This is what it feels like to burn from the inside on a cold Vermont night, bright as yolk against a sea of albumin, shut like a door, and sealed with duct tape. You know it's bad when people say, *You have your health*. I would rather have been shot. My father is a hunter. He has a good recipe for venison and dumplings and nothing but contempt for these nouveau butchers and chefs—the kind of men who pickle deer tongue and serve pork heart on a plate with rainbow chard and Brussels sprouts. *If these guys had any decency, they'd dig a hole out back and bury that pig's heart.* When I was nineteen my date held me face down in the water, my hands behind my back, and raped me—I think of it rarely, but the burnt taste of your tongue blisters my mouth every day. I want to believe in spring, in things that grow. Our daughter will dye Easter eggs, something that could have been a bird suddenly pink and impossible blue. The hyacinth bulbs in the soil will be faithful and true. And that pork heart asleep in the dirt, what will it do? Will it make a fist? Or bloom? Will it be reborn? Will it eat, grow strong, and then be led to slaughter?

Dream Charm

We are one part wish
and one part terror.

Deer Tongue

She wondered if a bird's wings could freeze midair. She wondered
what sheep felt during the shearing. You could say they made love in the cornfield
at the edge of the forest. The place where it all turned fallow and useless
as memory. *So what?* So there were red birds, and wool tights, and a plant not to be
touched. She was back in the forest, rubbing the fine hairs
of sumac between her fingers, against the crest of her cheek,
the branches doe-colored and soft, the red birds
feasting on berries that could kill a small child.

One afternoon in March her brother's best friend said, "Do you like these tights?"
ripping the seam between her legs. She liked looking up at the sky
and hearing the tear. She wondered if a bird's wings could freeze midair.
She chops the herbs for venison and dumplings,
sage, thyme, and tarragon.

There is a hunter and a church with twin crosses
at the top of the hill, pews worn and polished the color of brandy.
The wood is full of music, of an organ
and the prayers of those who have stopped
believing. She would like to make him more than words,
a three-berry pie and a pot of stew,
but she keeps her heart like a lost glove
tucked in her coat. Her shoulders are bare and breasts
white as doves that fly from a magician's cloak.
The red birds busy everywhere making nests out of hair
and the lost mittens of children. *So what?* What it would be like
to have her hands in his beard
and crush berries birds eat
between their tongues?

She folds and unfolds his handkerchief. This is what
the odd drawer is for. To open, to shut.
Some gifts we tie with ribbon,
some we deny. The body bleeds away
and what's left behind?

Antlers, the smooth and the hollow,
the white tail and a crystal eye, his tongue,
his tongue still speaking
inside her.

Crystal Charm
Honey,
stallion, larkspur,
throat.

Crewel

I'm busy. Blackberries everywhere.
The birch tree like a white queen among them,
the worker bees, the briars breeding furiously.
Look at that fat jewel, the bramble,
its blood sweet on my tongue.

I don't care what they say.

I can hear my mother in her pink halter top
laughing with the neighbor. Sun caught
in the ice of her tea sparkles across the lawn.
She wears cut-offs and her hair like a child,
two braids down the back.

In an hour or two I will be lost.

There is an old pickup knee-deep
in what's left of the creek.
Both doors rusted open as if
lovers fled the water seeping in
mid-kiss, a hand on her breast.
The lady's Sunday shoes and hem
of her best dress wet.

Oh prisoner, oh pretty miss.

I know something about wanting
like a kiss that cuts this way and that.
There is a nest of thorns
and a bird, a scavenger jay.

Blue as sky, as the veins singing
inside me, see how he stitches
all scratches and feathers,
his fine handiwork, *crewel*
like a ruby collar round my neck.

I want to make a pie. I want to eat
the whole wrecked world, peel
back the mottled pelt of the rabbit,
how tender its loins, *how tiny* its heart.

When you cry your eyes grow huge.
I watch the water pour
as if from a cup.

Close the car doors. Lock them shut.
Kiss me again and again. My thighs
berry, your nipples thorn.

My best dress is all wet.
The hem is torn. Someday
we will just be a story.

That's what I'm afraid of.

There was once a creek here,
a creek and an acre of blackberries.
There was. And there isn't
anymore.

II.

The History of Perfume

Pink poppies are capable of ruin, whole villages held hostage to blossom. Poachers are slaughtering musk deer by the thousand, ensnaring the male as he rubs against a tree. Can you imagine we're all just wandering in the forest? Leaving evidence of desire like a tear in a stocking? I want to write a poem about how you like to come—one hand on your own clit, one curled inside me. But that's private, isn't it? Sometimes when I kiss you goodbye, I'm trying to taste you. You drive away, and I've taken a bit of your DNA on my bottom lip into the house. In Belize we fought about abortion, and I left your cabana slamming the door. I waded into the water, wanting it over. When I showed up hours later, you pinned me to the floor. We drank the cool milk of coconuts that had fallen on your porch. You have a way with a machete. I picked frangipani and tucked it behind my ear. Maybe that flower belongs in a bottle. It's Christmas in New York, and the boys at the counter are exotic anemones and velvet orchids. They push L'Imperatrice, Flowerbomb, bottles of Poison. I pay good money for a flask of Guilty. Somewhere in Mongolia the deer are dying for us. You send me pictures of peonies to tattoo my back. The first time we made love I was afraid. The way your mouth was on me. My nipples bleeding into the next day. A perfumer is searching for persistence, for sillage. You inside me is the sound of a thousand doors unlocking. There are bottles spilling. Water floods the floor. I want to lie down in that field of poppies. In the forest I tell myself, *Don't be so obvious.*

Lesbian Charm
Votive,
areola, anchor,
tear.

Viola

Your hand took to my skin the way indigo takes to cotton. The bruise on my ass beautiful as a blackberry glistening wet in the white bowl, a posy of pansies, little faces lush with desire, velvet with trust. *Don't you dare close the curtains.* It was June, the afternoon ripening, the screen open as your hand. I thought you wanted me to be seen—wouldn't that add to my punishment?—but maybe it was you, wanting to risk unbuckling your belt. I mouth the black leather. I cut my lip. To be good is to wear the hawthorn crown, to bleed delicate as Miyuki beads. We necklace. We scatter so easily.

Whitetail

They're feeding while we sleep. Conifers, acorns, sweet clover. Crepuscular. They must tell each other stories in whatever tongue they speak. Each fawn makes its own distinct bleat. Does the mouth make a sound for gun, arrow, berry, or flee? Arrested between the bramble and the suburban street. Cars slide slowly as in a funeral processional. Our eyes meet. Who knows which way her children are? Or the lover she's running to—his velvet antlers unraveling? Flocked by the night, I want to slip inside her. Ears translucent in headlights, the white rings halo or ghostly bruise of eye. Front legs in the wood, hind on the concrete. It is so very hard to leave you. Mornings we made love my daughter was late for school. I would let her drink hot chocolate and watch TV. It's true I cared little for rules, for anything but you. At dusk, at dawn, I was in my pajamas. The buck hanging from the rafters of the garage. My mother took our picture, my hand on his flank. His coat faded red and still warm. Later I would refuse to eat his neck, then his heart. In that photograph, I am frozen. I am proud of what my father has done. I have not been so proud. I have opened my wounds for all the curious to see. I have wandered naked amongst engines and headlights. I have let you make a feast of me. How our favorite muscle can rage within its sea—one might name the ribs like the arc of a boat. But they call it a cage, don't they? Gun, arrow, berry, flee. I know these woods well. This way to the creek. This way—the massive pine split by lightning. North a field where you can find a brick cast by the old factory. I could point her to safety. I could whisper in those silken ears. I could taste her.

Midnight Charm

Foxglove,
leather, anise,
fur.

Llorando

When I awoke from the velvet screen,
I was not the one. I have never
been for you. This might be love,
but that was not a kiss, just a woman
lip-synching in a carmine dress.
We crash. We spark bright
in the night. The tear

appliqued on my cheek
is only crystal, but a ring of real diamonds
burns a hole deep in my heart.
I don't understand coal
or carbon, but this knot
of want, I practice
until my fingers bleed. Bite

by bite or grace of knife,
I am weary of my own beauty
and the way it invites pain—slice, shave,
filet. Shiny synonyms for eviscerate.
Your chest feathered
blue and vermillion,
circles above me raptor,
rapture it's all

an illusion. *There is no band,*
but we hear a band. My eyes
painted the color of sirens,
I too can fly away.
I can hurt you with my mouth.
Will you please

separate the water
from the salt? Wash me away,
make a tiny tear
gleam like the galaxy.
Remember nothing
or too much.

Velocity

Open the tiny lockets of Bleeding Hearts, I want to be buried alive under a pile of petals, and clothe my sex in a stitch of Queen Anne's Lace. It's Jacaranda. That's the purple we loved, adorning the branches of Lisbon. But now I will never see the cherry blossoms of your Kyoto. Or pick frangipani again in Belize. All the flowers we traveled. The roadside bouquets and stone fruit pies of the Northeast. The air is choking, the throat is sweet. *Oh rose hips, oh sticky peach.* I try to explain our apocalypse. I knew I was playing with fire. I don't say I would do it again and again. We forage in the woods for what is delicious and what is poison. How could you have been any brighter? You picked nutmeg, you ground cardamom into my tea with your bare hands, placed a curl of cinnamon by the bed. When I was nine a wisp of a girl moved next door. At dusk she would strip to her panties and pink camisole and lie down in the middle of the street—her small, near-nakedness a kind of beacon, a siren calling to cars come closer. Her faith a kind of patient wound. I couldn't stop watching. Did you ever notice the root of hurtling is hurt? That's what I think every time I speed down the highway, forced to skip the exit that would lead me to your house. The highway on which I counted five dead deer this summer. Always belly up, the white pelt like a flag, the body surrendered. My long-legged, stunned sisters. Those headlights coming over them like desire.

Quiet Charm

Listen,
lisianthus, apology,
apology.

Collision

You were not as I had imagined in the ones that came before—the poems in which I conjured you, dreaming *darling girl, stunned sister.* You flew at me like a kiss, a hard slap upon the hood of my car. Behind the wheel I could see the soft curl of white on your belly, the slit of your sex, the coal of hooves, so close, for a second, as if you were nursing at my breast. Then you were off, leaping defiantly. I'm now the one on the highway shaking, the cars speeding by. My skirt flying up in the wind and you, *wild thing,* are not my metaphor. But this doesn't stop me from following you into the switchgrass and sweet clover, the thousand little tongues of lupine tasting. Who needs taxonomy? We are all invasive and beautiful. We are too many. Look for the tender birches, for blackberries. The corn stalks crushed soft as linen. They are gathering. The does and their fawns. I see now you are younger than my own daughter. And you are bleeding. If I take off my shoes and shed my dress, may I lay down beside you? What do I have to offer, but my skin and hair to poultice you? I mean to do penance. I understand the wound, how it calls to you. It asks to breathe, and it is a kind of song that can't help singing. You've read the poems. You've known all along. I too have bolted when I shouldn't have, thrown myself in front of a car.

Pocket Charm

Scarab,
cherry, linen,
chalk.

Vow

Sometimes I think walking the dog
at night is a kind of penance
or prayer. The moon slivers and glows
bone white. I am a woman who sleeps
alone with a creature beside her
like the nun with the little yellow bird
in a cage. Bernadette? Benedicte?
I don't remember, but my grandmother
brought me to visit. I wondered
at her title *Sister*, but now I think
I understand. Taking shelter
in a long black dress and the hand of God,
she can still taste the world
outside her.

III.

Transubstantiation

What if I held the dead rabbit in my arms and massaged his tiny heart,

what if he leapt into the field

and returned to the bramble and sweet clover?

What if I gathered your ex-wife's pills, ground them into snow

and made angels in the backyard?

What if for a moment there was laughter?

What if I led her flock of secret lovers into the light,

kissed them each goodnight,

swaddled them in crochet and tucked them in a drawer?

What if there was always hot water?

What I emptied all your father's bottles into the river, what if he was baptized

in those waters, what if we made a boat of wild irises and reeds

and delivered him into the next world?

What if we unlocked all the doors? What if we took the doors off the hinges?

What if I fed your sisters soft bread? What if they could look in the mirror

and see love between women and be full of gratitude for tenderness?

What if I put my tongue between their legs?

What if shame flowed out of them and shimmered?

What if they could be blessed by radical love?

What if I gathered all the guns in your house and took each barrel into my mouth?

What if the bullets exploded like a host of sparrows?

What if they disappeared into the sky?

What if they named a new constellation?

What if I washed the floors and the nine other faces?

What if I gathered fiddleheads and pickled them?

What if I boiled the syrup and slaughtered the hog?

What if I burned my eyes by the light and bloodied my fingers

so she could go to your crib as she wanted to, so she could lift you,

so she might unbutton her blouse and put your lips to her breast?

And sit for a while.

And this would be the first knowledge,

this would be.

Necklace Charm
Scapula,
cobalt, lacquer,
clove.

Lilacs

Admittedly, I know nothing about being twenty and pregnant,

                         a young wife in rural America, nothing.

All the purple ghosts breathing and blossoming,

stroller wheels, dirt roads   only your hands ghost beauty above me.

All the roads we traveled Skunk Hollow, Sand Hill.   My lover,

   the youngest of ten, worries, *You never speak about your childhood.*

                   My own daughter says, *I can't picture it.*

But I am your daughter, and this is our story: lilacs,

               a hydrangea tree, and a place called the egg farm.

There was a shallow river we waded in with a herd cooling downstream,

            the dairy across a long field of clover. You were beautiful

with two braids, and a pink halter top tied like a sling. How could I know

          you would always be absent? Years later when I asked

you would spit at me, your face a violence,

words like *adoption, abortion,* flesh open

against the electric fence. *Abortion.*

The lilacs like a row of postulants.   *Adoption.*

Lilacs like child brides, unbearably sweet,

their girl babies forever accidental, birthed in the old wood,

feral and inflorescent.

Birthday Altar at Forty-Nine

If you wish to honor the gods, you may
roll out a mat before the altar
and lay flat on your belly. The pain
of the past will be collected
like the seeds of the columbine
your mother pinched from the dead
into her palm. You will be all husk,
perhaps if you're lucky a few loose threads
of silk will stick. Sweaty with glisten,
you are an apprentice to shame.
Remember how you taught yourself to masturbate?
I mean really come all spectacle, all fancy
reading Anaïs Nin. Stupid girl, cosseted in white
and so faithful you were gullible,
but here all along is the gift of your own body.
Believe in this field endless and immaculate:
tactile and soft as spiked millet,
your nipples pink as the dawn,
sex flocked with soft tendrils
of strawberry blonde. Novitiate,
not now. Never again. No
more.

Butterfly Charm

If you put your tongue to my breasts
The ribs will crack open. See the lungs—
One rustling like a butterfly wing, the other
a side of beef.

Sacrament

I tried to love the sacrament of loneliness. Burnt and burnished, I bowed my head and took nothing into my mouth. Shards of quartz and bits of tar scarred the soft flesh of my feet, but I knew at the end of the road there was a field, and suddenly I was standing in you. At your temple a forgotten orchard winesap and russet sweet. The barred owl your mother cared for nests there. The one that flew with a broken wing from her arm and back to its cage each evening. My hand runs the length of the field, and the field *is* your torso, odd rib that caught my heart like a lacy hem. We larkspur, we garland coreopsis. We plow and we harrow. We pasture spikelets of timothy, foxtail, sunflowers—the sap on their seed like my own mouth shameless. Eight years I lived inside prayer, imprisoned in a locket. Your lips unlock me. *Radiant one,* I want to be the seed to your sparrow. Your song is diligent and wild. You bare-breasted above me. This season pleasure is my new constant, my almanac. We carve our names into hickory like a headboard. Tiny boats of milkweed set sail. I sew a pillow with the stuff. We glisten against wool. We are not fallow. We gather our hands and bow our heads. There is a table and bounty. We vesper, and I am astonished.

Passionem

The elevator opened and there you were, holding two cups of coffee and a paper bag of scones. That's how I remember the hallway, clean and bleak as a bone. Your neck smelling faintly of coconut and perhaps gardenia or frangipani. I don't know if I smelled like the floor of the ICU or the body of my dead father. He was not cold as they said he would be. I climbed in his bed and put my head on his chest and my hand on his belly which was still warm and soft. Only later when you took me to the Vatican, standing in front of the Pietà did I think of his arms, still the muscled arms of an athlete and felt them cold and hard like marble. It is impossible to separate the body of the Virgin from her child, but what I can tell you is she was thankful for the lost thorn which scratched her cheek because from that moment on she was bleeding. I want to get married, and I wanted my father to walk me down the aisle. I was never his property, but we are kept by the ones we love. He kept me and my daughter. Safe for many years. We were lost, and when we needed shelter, he took us in. I was lost in the Pietà. Later I heard your voice on my headset telling our guide, "I've lost Eve. I can't find her." My father died before I got to care for him as one cares for their child. *Keep me.* The long hallway was in a way our aisle. You appeared. None of us in white. A bouquet of thorns. How could I be anywhere but your body? My father's body delivering me to you.

Blood Charm

Nape,
cloak, cassia,
float.

Intercession

The virus swirls too close to the day of your death. The principal of your granddaughter's school suggests *a day of intention,* suggests we pray to the Patron Saint of Respiratory Illnesses, Saint Bernardine of Siena. As you know, I'm not what Greta calls "a devote," but for a moment I flush with guilt. If I had only known of Siena, I might have saved you with prayer. As if we all pray to Saint Bernardine the ventilators will appear in hospitals like manna, the ventilators of five loaves and two fishes. As if fevers will cool and the flocks of children will be back at their desks. Good student, I research Saint Bernardine, maker of monograms, an ugly nobleman renowned not only for scrubbing hospital floors, but for his intolerance, for slapping the blasphemous amongst the fruit and cattle of the marketplace. Saint Bernardine would not have saved you with his cruelty or hereditary wealth, qualities you despise in our reckless leader. I avoid the news, and I hate the word *ventilator* everywhere, the way that machine broke your body like a horse, you needing both to breathe and to escape. And me on my knees, praying only to you, my father, your blue eyes shut, the hair on your arms almost sparkling under the bright stars of the ICU. Tell me, who is the patron saint of adult daughters of the dying? Who would hear me, over the ventilator, weeping?

Rope Charm

Bruise,
buoy, violet,
pulse.

The Pantheon

I could almost touch the sparrows balancing on the perimeter of the dome.
The gloss of tiny eyes, feathers, barbules and plume.
The kitchen window almost all I remember—
there were velvet curtains the color of lemons,
a bidet I didn't use. I cut my ankle shaving in the narrow shower.
I don't remember sleeping in the bed with my lover, but I must have.
I don't remember putting the soft cured meats into my mouth or drinking wine,
but I must have. It's still there—
the great oculus, a temple to a goddess so old
it became a church to a god. Hadrian
and his Romans did what your doctors could not.

How could a strange city you never traveled to be so full of your body?
Antiquity's a blur. That May I dragged my grief like a fresh kill
through every piazza in Rome. Bloody like those antlered creatures
you shot and dressed in the forests of home.
A good daughter I ate them all—venison, elk, moose. I made you stew.
I studied Latin, but even here—we don't pray the Latin mass.

Deus, Deus meus.

Why should your body be here and this square full of your soul?
Early in the morning the brides come to twirl by the fountain.
The photographers on their knees like the devoted, the way
we prayed on the hospital floor.
There's one girl in red. She is impenitent.
Her long taffeta train like petals of a begonia or the mouth of a wound.
I decide her dress is my heart. My heart dressed
and eaten in the field.

Star Charm
Gossamer,
scythe, stain,
crown.

Loveland

Your cheekbones, wrists so delicate when sleeping. We drift
in the fog's silver bloom. Derelict boats. Sail-less. No pink Cupcake this year.
So blue, so hazy. The blue flowered shorts, mesmerizing Meconopsis.

Hypnotic.

The poet reading, her whole body rising, a strange shock of beauty.
Tiny little lights, twinkling.
I love the way the host sways *oh honey, ladies*
sometimes queerness is a singing, a secret song.
There's that poem by Mark, *Put it on,*
it's the only thing we have to wear.

The dog on Pearl is blind, but we're both held by birds,
the seagulls clearly up to something—what's that book, by a medieval monk?
All birds, mammals, even the whales are a *clutch, a harem,*
a coven, a charm. Remember John Clare? You were going to read him.
You were the wind, you were far beyond, already living your next life,
the sea gulls were there too. I think about that with my dad.
Greta said, *You said Pa Pa Mike is watching over me, but where is he?*
I've been trying. I've been trying, and I can't feel him. Yesterday for a second
I thought I saw him ordering a mojito at the pool. He seemed happy,
at ease among all the boys, chiseled and glittering.

You said I wouldn't kiss you. That's not true. I have refused
a thousand times. It's true. I get so angry. It's all or nothing. Not kissing or
I can't stop kissing you. I know you worry
for your son, his lips unloved. His heart leans
toward sorrow. The clematis pink into purple.
The yellow corona like eyelashes, the sun you want so badly,
the secret, coming out. Pride. Carnival.
We make our own holidays. *I'll Be Your Mirror,*
your ass so good babe, in your new Levi's.

Heaven is a Place on Earth, Just like Heaven.
Say a Little Prayer for You. You like that I can't quite let go
of the Church. Your ex-wife did not believe.
Could faith have something to do with faithful?

Miraculosa.

Saint Mary's of the Harbor. Let's get married here, babe.
You can tell your sisters the Episcopalians are just like the Catholics,
but friendlier. I have never thought you walked on water.
I've just arrived, and you are here in this place,
hands in your pockets. The bees quiet in their yellow house,

the one peony half-open,
its pink unfinished, waiting
to receive them.

Paper Charm
Pearl,
orchid, lantern,
cuff.

Wing

If an apple holds enough of a star, the loon wears a red cravat.
We practice their call over the phone. The loon's eye red as an apple.
Our eyes scan the shore, seduced, *sanctuary, hatchling, brood.*
Seduced we believe we could speak their strange language.
The red was inside, Mt. Elan burning
inside me. The gold glowed like honeycomb, plucked from the jar.
What does it mean to speak the same language? How many times have I said,
We don't work, oil and water. How many times have you said,
I'm done. But what if a bird is a promise? What if
place makes its own vernacular? Let me make a map.
Let our tongues be flecked with gold. *Lakehouse, loon.*
Tongue and groove. Tell me everything you know
about pine and how to heat with a wood stove, and I'll tell you
how the water flows. Put a kettle on the stove,
lay me down in a bed of feathers. Red cross-stitch
wing above our bed, the red of the loon
is a thread we unravel.

Lady's Charm

The history of love folds into itself
like an accordion. Smooth
the silk pleats of my skirt.

Nest

Let it be enough: this fall too
I carry my heart. Every morning
it's a ceremony: I make coffee.
I count the birds: a ritual
of cardinals, two
in the spruce. Three
sparrows on the stop sign.

       Pileated, red breast, thrush.

At night I wash my hair and consider
the blue veins of my breasts
in the mirror, drag my hand
across the levee, locks empty
and pour inside me.

Every time I'm driving home
alone, north on 91,
a hawk appears beside the road.
We lock eyes. I wear this key
around my neck forever,
fist of feathers, my father.
I'm not just making metaphor again,
the bird is not a symbol of wanting. My father
copper-winged, a good man,
he deserved a better death.

Hair comes out in my hands.
I release it—out the window, some bird
will make use of it, to bind
love to their breast. Loss
is muddled with this land.

My friend Bill the photographer
tells me about the edge
of a prison yard scattered
with graves and birdhouses.

Creatures live there
voluntarily. I did not believe
this would happen to me.
I wear no one's ring.
I know the name
of every tree.

Notes

"Llorando" (pg. 28) is inspired by a scene in David Lynch's *Mulholland Drive*. Rebekah Del Rio performs a Spanish version of Roy Orbison's "Crying." *"There is no band, but we hear a band"* is a quote from the film.

"Loveland" (pg. 51) contains a line from Mark Doty's poem "Esta Noche."

Eve Alexandra's first book *The Drowned Girl* was selected by C.K. Williams for the Stan and Tom Wick Poetry Prize. Alexandra's poems have appeared in publications such as *Narrative, Barrow Street, Cape Cod Review, Harvard Review*, and *American Poetry Review.* She teaches creative writing and literature at the University of Vermont.

Publications by Two Sylvias Press:

The Daily Poet: Day-By-Day Prompts For Your Writing Practice
by Kelli Russell Agodon and Martha Silano (Print and eBook)

The Daily Poet Companion Journal (Print)

Everything is Writable: 240 Poetry Prompts from Two Sylvias Press
by Kelli Russell Agodon and Annette Spaulding-Convy (Print)

Demystifying the Manuscript: Essays and Interviews on Creating a Book of Poems
edited by Susan Rich and Kelli Russell Agodon (Print)

Fire On Her Tongue: An Anthology of Contemporary Women's Poetry
edited by Kelli Russell Agodon and Annette Spaulding-Convy (Print and eBook)

The Poet Tarot and Guidebook: A Deck Of Creative Exploration (Print)

The Inspired Poet: Writing Exercises to Spark New Work
by Susan Landgraf (Print)

None of Us in White, Winner of the 2023 Two Sylvias Press Wilder Prize
by Eve Alexandra (Print)

Letters, Unwritten, Winner of the 2023 Two Sylvias Press Chapbook Prize
by Andrew Robin (Print)

Horns, Winner of the 2022 Two Sylvias Press Wilder Prize
by Tiffany Midge (Print)

The Call of Paradise, Winner of the 2022 Two Sylvias Press Chapbook Prize
by Majda Gama (Print)

Omena Bay Testament, Winner of the 2021 Two Sylvias Press Wilder Prize
by Gail Griffin (Print)

At Night My Body Waits, Winner of the 2021 Two Sylvias Press Chapbook Prize
by Saúl Hernández (Print)

Nightmares & Miracles, Winner of the 2020 Two Sylvias Press Wilder Prize
by Michelle Bitting (Print)

Hallucinating a Homestead, Winner of the 2020 Two Sylvias Press
Chapbook Prize by Meg E. Griffitts (Print)

Shade of Blue Trees, Finalist 2019 Two Sylvias Press Wilder Prize
by Kelly Cressio-Moeller (Print)

Disappearing Queen, Winner of the 2019 Two Sylvias Press Wilder Prize
by Gail Martin (Print)

Deathbed Sext, Winner of the 2019 Two Sylvias Press Chapbook Prize
by Christopher Salerno (Print)

Crown of Wild, Winner of the 2018 Two Sylvias Press Wilder Prize
by Erica Bodwell (Print)

American Zero, Winner of the 2018 Two Sylvias Press Chapbook Prize
by Stella Wong (Print and eBook)

All Transparent Things Need Thundershirts, Winner of the 2017 Two Sylvias Press
Wilder Prize by Dana Roeser (Print and eBook)

Where The Horse Takes Wing: The Uncollected Poems of Madeline DeFrees
edited by Anne McDuffie (Print and eBook)

In The House Of My Father, Winner of the 2017 Two Sylvias Press Chapbook Prize
by Hiwot Adilow (Print and eBook)

Box, Winner of the 2017 Two Sylvias Press Poetry Prize
by Sue D. Burton (Print and eBook)

Tsigan: The Gypsy Poem (New Edition)
by Cecilia Woloch (Print and eBook)

PR For Poets
by Jeannine Hall Gailey (Print and eBook)

Appalachians Run Amok, Winner of the 2016 Two Sylvias Press Wilder Prize
by Adrian Blevins (Print and eBook)

Pass It On! by Gloria J. McEwen Burgess (Print)

Killing Marias
by Claudia Castro Luna (Print and eBook)

The Ego and the Empiricist, Finalist 2016 Two Sylvias Press Chapbook Prize
by Derek Mong (Print and eBook)

The Authenticity Experiment
by Kate Carroll de Gutes (Print and eBook)

Mytheria, Finalist 2015 Two Sylvias Press Wilder Prize
by Molly Tenenbaum (Print and eBook)

Arab in Newsland , Winner of the 2016 Two Sylvias Press Chapbook Prize
by Lena Khalaf Tuffaha (Print and eBook)

The Blue Black Wet of Wood, Winner of the 2015 Two Sylvias Press Wilder Prize
by Carmen R. Gillespie (Print and eBook)

Fire Girl: Essays on India, America, and the In-Between
by Sayantani Dasgupta (Print and eBook)

Blood Song
by Michael Schmeltzer (Print and eBook)

Community Chest
by Natalie Serber (Print)

Naming The No-Name Woman,
Winner of the 2015 Two Sylvias Press Chapbook Prize by Jasmine An (Print and eBook)

Phantom Son: A Mother's Story of Surrender
by Sharon Estill Taylor (Print and eBook)

What The Truth Tastes Like
by Martha Silano (Print and eBook)

landscape/heartbreak
by Michelle Peñaloza (Print and eBook)

Earth, Winner of the 2014 Two Sylvias Press Chapbook Prize
by Cecilia Woloch (Print and eBook)

The Cardiologist's Daughter
by Natasha Kochicheril Moni (Print and eBook)

She Returns to the Floating World
by Jeannine Hall Gailey (Print and eBook)

Hourglass Museum
by Kelli Russell Agodon (eBook)

Cloud Pharmacy
by Susan Rich (eBook)

Dear Alzheimer's: A Caregiver's Diary & Poems
by Esther Altshul Helfgott (eBook)

Listening to Mozart: Poems of Alzheimer's
by Esther Altshul Helfgott (eBook)

The Wilder Series Poetry Book Prize

The Wilder Series Book Prize is an annual contest hosted by Two Sylvias Press. It is open to women over 50 years of age (established or emerging poets) and includes a $1000 prize, publication by Two Sylvias Press, 20 copies of the winning book, and a vintage, art nouveau pendant. Women submitting manuscripts may be poets with one or more previously published chapbooks/books or poets without any prior chapbook/book publications. The judges for the prize are Two Sylvias Press cofounders and coeditors, Kelli Russell Agodon and Annette Spaulding-Convy.

The Wilder Series Book Prize Winners and Finalists

2023: Eve Alexandra, *None of Us in White* (Winner)

2022: Tiffany Midge, *Horns* (Winner)

2021: Gail Griffin, *Omena Bay Testament* (Winner)

2020: Michelle Bitting, *Nightmares & Miracles* (Winner)

2019: Gail Martin, *Disappearing Queen* (Winner)
Kelly Cressio-Moeller, *Shade of Blue Trees* (Finalist)

2018: Erica Bodwell, *Crown of Wild* (Winner)

2017: Dana Roeser, *All Transparent Things Need Thundershirts* (Winner)

2016: Adrian Blevins, *Appalachians Run Amok* (Winner)

2015: Carmen R. Gillespie, *The Blue Black Wet of Wood* (Winner)
Molly Tenenbaum, *Mytheria* (Finalist)

www.ingramcontent.com/pod-product-compliance
Lightning Source LLC
Chambersburg PA
CBHW031148090426
42738CB00008B/1259